A CENTURY OF SERVICE

A Brief History of the North Congregational Church

Amherst, Massachusetts

1826-1926

North Congregational Church

HERITAGE BOOKS
2009

HERITAGE BOOKS
AN IMPRINT OF HERITAGE BOOKS, INC.

Books, CDs, and more—Worldwide

For our listing of thousands of titles see our website
at
www.HeritageBooks.com

A Facsimile Reprint
Published 2009 by
HERITAGE BOOKS, INC.
Publishing Division
100 Railroad Ave. #104
Westminster, Maryland 21157

Originally published
Press of Carpenter & Morehouse
Amherst, Massachusetts
1927

— Publisher's Notice —
In reprints such as this, it is often not possible to remove blemishes from the original. We feel the contents of this book warrant its reissue despite these blemishes and hope you will agree and read it with pleasure.

International Standard Book Numbers
Paperbound: 978-0-7884-2872-2
Clothbound: 978-0-7884-7580-1

Pastors of Church.

Rev. William W. Hunt	1827-1837	Rev. George F. Humphrey	1875-1875
Rev. George Cook	1839-1852	Rev. Dwight W. Marsh	1876-1878
Rev. George E. Fisher	1852-1858	Rev. George H. Johnson	1879-1888
Rev. John W. Underhill	1859-1862	Rev. Eber W. Gaylord	1890-1902
Rev. S. O. Dyer	1864-1865	Rev. John P. Manwell	1902-1907
Rev. Daniel S. Rogan	1865-1866	Rev. Byron F. Gustin	1908-1922
Rev. William D. Herrick	1867-1874	Rev. Frank C. Seymour	1922-

Deacons of Church.

Daniel Russell, Jr.	1826-1839	Fred S. Cooley	1899-1907
Ranson Dickinson	1826-1890	Alpheus Crocker	1907-1922
Austin Loomis	1839-1861	Frank W. Harrington	1908-1911
Lyman Smith	1840-1845	Robert J. Goldberg	1909-1918
Edward Graves	1861-1866	W. Lowell Roberts	1911-1916
Levi Russell	1845-1855	Howard A. Parsons	1911-1926
Samuel N. White	1845-1852	Frank N. Dickinson	1912-
Charles H. Bangs	1855-1872	Walter W. Chenoweth	1916-
Edmund Hobart	1866-1908	Edwin H. Dickinson	1918-
Samuel E. Harrington	1871-1915	Alfred O. Tower	1925-
Asa Adams	1872-1910	Fred S. Cooley	1926-
George L. Cooley	1872-1925		

Superintendents of Sunday School.

Daniel Dickinson	1827	Charles H. Kellogg	1869-1875
Benjamin Schneider	1828 *Students at*	George L. Cooley	1876-1880
Stillman Pratt	1829 *Amh. Coll.*	B. Franklin Kellogg	1881-1885
Daniel Dickinson		Charles H. Kellogg	1886-1896
Levi Russell		Howard A. Parsons	1897-1904
Samuel White		Fred S. Cooley	1905-1906
Lyman Gunn		Howard A. Parsons	1907-1917
Eben P. Spear		Robert J. Goldberg	1918
Albert W. Ball		Howard A. Parsons	1918-1922
Reuben Roberts		John G. Archibald	1923-1924
Edmund Hobart		George F. Pushee	1925-
Marshall B. Cushman			

HISTORICAL SKETCH

Early in the settlement of Amherst the First Church was organized, and in 1872 part of the congregation withdrew and formed the Second Church at East Street. Until 1824 the people from all over the town attended these two churches, going on horse back, in "fall back chaises" or on foot. The Dickinson boys who lived at the City, now Cushman, on the road to Leverett, walked to the East Amherst Church bare-foot carrying their shoes, over the road now known as East Street, stopping just before they arrived at the church to put them on. This was to save the wear of their shoes.

In 1824 the South Amherst Church was built and the people at the north part of the town began to think about a Meeting House. Rev. Daniel Clark was invited in 1825 to preach in the school house at the "City". June 8, 1826 fifty-nine persons met in North Amherst and formed an organization called "The Congregational Union Society of Amherst." They began to talk about building a Meeting House; but the question was, how could it be supported? Oliver Dickinson started a subscription paper for a fund, the income to be used for the support of a minister, and $3355.35 was raised. There was quite a controversy as to where the Meeting House should be located. The "City" folks wanted it on the corner of Pine Street and East Pleasant Street. The rest of the Parish on the location where it now stands. Joseph Cowls would give the land if it was there. Where was the money coming from to build? Oliver Dickinson again came to the front and said the church should be built on the Cowls land and he would build it himself. Labor and material were contributed. Stones for the foundation were drawn from Pelham by yokes of oxen. In due season the corner-stone was laid by the Rev. Mr. Perkins of East Amherst. In this corner-stone was placed a box, the contents of which are unknown.

The raising was a gala occasion for the whole country around. "A good and decent entertainment" was furnished for all. Capt. Winthrop Clapp of Montague was paid $2900.00 by Mr. Dickinson for building the Church. Mr. Dickinson sold the pews for from $50. to $75. taking farm produce or anything in payment. One man gave a pair of oxen, and a few gave money. He deeded the pews to the purchasers and in this way he was partly repaid for his money invested in the Church. November 15, 1826 the Church was dedicated. The same day the Council met at the house of Mr. Joseph Cowls and forty-seven people presented letters of dismission and recommendation and were recognized as a Church of Christ.

The Meeting House was built with a gallery running around all four sides and a round box-like pulpit, on a level with galleries, was hung at the west side. The minister entered a door on the north side and climbed a narrow stairway. When seated he was entirely hidden from his people.

Rev. Mr. Hunt preached the first Sabbath after the dedication and was pastor until his death in 1837. In the summer of 1831 there was a great revival. The farmers left their haying and attended meetings lasting for four successive days. At this time Mr. Dickinson gave a deed of the Church to the Parish. From his salary of $450. Mr. Hunt gave a subscription toward the silver communion service which was purchased about this time.

Stoves were put in the Meeting House in 1835, one on each side at the west end with pipes going the whole length of the aisles to chimneys at the east side. One person still living remembers a Sunday morning when one of the pipes separated during the service, and fell hitting a Mr. Smith on the head, causing quite a commotion. A furnace took the place of stoves in 1892.

The second pastor was Rev. George Cook who came as a young man of twenty-eight with a bride of eighteen. For him the parsonage was built from plans he drew. During his time the pulpit was moved to the east end of the church. The Parish House was also built from his plans, jointly by the Town and Parish. The first floor was used as a school-house until the Parish bought the building in 1869. Mr. Cook left in 1852 because of the failure of his health, much to the regret of the people.

Rev. G. E. Fisher followed and was pastor for five years. During that time one hundred and thirty-two united with the Church.

Rev. John Underhill's pastorate was of only three years duration, his death coming at the parsonage Oct. 17, 1862. $1232 was

Know all Men by these Presents, that I Oliver Dickinson of Amherst in the County of Hampshire and Common Wealth of Massachusetts yeoman being sole Proprietor of a Meeting house lately erected at the North Part of the Town of Amherst near the house of Joseph Cowls

in consideration of the sum of two hundred & seventy five dollars and cents paid me by Jonathan Cowls of Amherst in the County of Hampshire the receipt whereof I do hereby acknowledge, do by these presents, grant, bargain and sell, and convey to the said Jon. Cowls heirs and assigns five certain Pew in said Meeting-house, situated on the lower floor, and numbered 48-24-21-25 & 55 To have and to hold the same with all the privileges and appurtenances thereto belonging to him the said Cowls his heirs and assigns forever.

Provided however, that if the said grantee his heirs or assigns or any person or persons claiming under them or either of them, shall allow the said Pew or Pews to be painted or suffer any alteration thereof to be made affecting its exterior appearance without the permission of a majority of the Proprietors of said House; or shall let the said pew or any part thereof to any negro or mullatto or in any way admit any negro or mullatto to the possession or occupancy of the same, then the said Pew or Pews or such share thereof so let or occupied shall in every such case be forfeited and become the property of the other proprietors of said Meeting-house.

In witness whereof I have hereunto set my hand and seal this twenty ninth day of November in the year of our Lord one thousand eight hundred and twenty six

Signed, Sealed and delivered in presence of us,

Charles Cooley
Caleb Hubbard

Oliver Dickinson

A Century of Service.

raised in 1860 for repairing the Church. Rev. S. O. Dyer was acting pastor for one year.

Rev. Daniel H. Rogan, whose wife was a daughter of Mr. Hunt the first pastor, served the Church one year, 1865-1866.

The sixth man to be called by the Church was Rev. Wm. D. Herrick. He came in 1867 and left to go to Gardner in 1874. There were two revivals during his time with an addition of seventy-three members.

Rev. George F. Humphrey's was the shortest pastorate, being less than a year. Rev. D. W. Marsh was acting pastor for two years 1876-1878. During this time the Church celebrated its fiftieth anniversary.

In 1879 $1471 was spent in repairing the Church. It was at this time that the old forty-eight-pained windows were replaced by the four-light ones now there.

Rev. George H. Johnson came in 1879 directly from the seminary to his first pastorate and soon brought his bride to the parsonage. The ten years of his service were fruitful, ninety-eight being added to the Church. The Christian Endeavor Society was organized and was very flourishing. He left for a better position and Mr. Herrick, having moved to Amherst to live, acted as pastor until Rev. E. W. Gaylord came in 1890. Mr. Gaylord was a grandson of Ransom Dickinson, one of the first deacons of the Church. His deep love for the Church and devotion to its interests were very marked and helped the success of his work. It was just before he came that Mrs. Fisher gave the pipe organ to the Church in memory of her father, mother and daughter. The parsonage was also thoroughly repaired and enlarged. Nov. 15, 1901 the Diamond Jubilee was held. Many of the sons and daughters of the first members were present and one, Mr. Ransom Cowls, remembered the laying of the corner stone and had known every pastor of the Church. It was a very enthusiastic gathering and was an inspiration to the members to go forward with the work their fathers had started.

Rev. John P. Manwell came in 1902 and was here five years. During this time the interior of the Church was redecorated and electric lights installed. Dr. C. S. Walker of Amherst acted as pastor until Rev. B. F. Gustin came in 1908. His pastorate was longer than any of the others—fourteen years. They were years of devoted service on his part with ninety-three additions to the Church. It was during this time that the Church lost three faithful officers, Edmund Hobart, Samuel Harrington, and Asa Adams, who served as Deacons respectively for forty-two, forty-four and thirty-eight years. Deacon George L. Cooley, who served with these three, passed on in 1925 after fifty-three years of active service for the Church he so much loved.

In the summer of 1922, the present pastor Rev. Frank C. Seymour came to the Church, another young man directly from the seminary, filled with a deep desire to do his Heavenly Father's work. The additions to the Church since he came have been sixty-eight. In 1924 Parish Hall was repaired and a furnace installed.

Nov. 13-14-15, 1927 the Centennial Anniversary was celebrated. Saturday evening a reception and exhibit was held at Parish Hall. The room was filled with people, many from out of town. Mrs. G. D. Jones and her committee had a very interesting collection of pictures, books and papers. A few of the most important in connection with the Church were the deed of the pulpit, the deed of a pew, the sermon preached by Mr. Hunt at the wedding of Oliver Dickinson, the Church Treasurer's first book, the first Church Manuel with names of first members, and pictures of many of the first members. A short program of music was given and several people told stories of early days. Refreshments were served and all enjoyed the meeting of old friends.

Sunday morning the Centennial Sermon was preached by Rev. Frederick Harlan Page, D.D., of Waltham—"One Hundred Years" —Text: Deut. 32-27. Mr. Seymour, in the Children's Sermon, told the story of the building of the Church. Special music was furnished by the choir. The Lord's Supper was served. In the evening was given a concert—"Glimpses of A Century of Church Music." Rev. Mr. Gustin read a paper written by Mrs. F. S. Cooley. A chorus directed by Mr. Francis B. Gustin, illustrated this by music of the different periods. The costumes of the singers dated from one hundred years ago to the present day and made the effect very realistic.

HISTORICAL PROGRAM

CENTENNIAL DAY
Monday afternoon, November 15, at 2.00 o'clock

DEACON FRED S. COOLEY, Presiding

Organ Prelude: Pilgrim Chorus from Tannhauser, *Wagner*
    EDITH PARKER EASTMAN

Historical Facts of a Century,
    F. S. COOLEY

Neighbors of North Amherst at Amherst Center
    JOHN M. TYLER

Quintette: Hark, Hark My Soul! *Shelley*
    HAZEL HASKINS, EUNICE SEYMOUR, CLARA DICKINSON
    CLARK THAYER, FRANCIS GUSTIN

Presentation of Portrait of Oliver Dickinson by RAYMOND DICKINSON, Acceptance by REV. FRANK C. SEYMOUR.

Early History of North Amherst Church,
    REV. GEORGE H. JOHNSON, Cleveland, Ohio

Hymn No. 444,
    While with Ceaseless Course the Sun, *S. Webbe 1792*

Why the Fathers Planted a Church in North Amherst
    REV. JOHN P. MANWELL, Williamsburg, Mass.

The Challenge,
    REV. BYRON F. GUSTIN

Organ Postlude, Maich *Hill Shelley*
    GRACE C. COOLEY

    A supper was served in the Hall with Prof. A. A. MacKimmie as Toastmaster.

    The last event on the program was the presenting in the Church of the play "The Rich Young Man" under the direction of the Religious Drama Committee—Mrs. F. C. Seymour, Rev. B. F. Gustin, and Mrs. Lillian Sanborn. It was very finely rendered and very impressive; a fitting close to a successful celebration.

GLIMPSES OF A CENTURY OF CHURCH MUSIC

Mrs. F. S. Cooley

To understand the development of church music in the past century a brief survey of previous conditions in America is necessary.

Two diverse influences worked in Protestant music. Martin Luther an ardent musician who used hymn book, choir, and congregational singing on one hand, and on the other, John Calvin, a bitter opponent of the fine arts, who reduced the practice of music among his followers to psalms sung in unison. He said, "Those songs and melodies which are composed for the mere pleasure of the ear, and all they call ornamental music and songs for four parts do not behoove the majesty of the church and cannot fail greatly to displease God". Calvin wanted the music of the church to attract no attention to itself but to merely be a peg on which to hang a rythmic recitation of the psalms. It was this Calvinist lead that our Pilgrim fathers followed and that moulded the earliest music of New England.

Both Pilgrim Plymouth and Puritan Boston while differing on doctrinal points, united in their distrust of music. It would have been abolished but for the undoubted fact that the Hebrews employed psalm singing in their religious worship, so they did allow the singing of *two* psalms, while rejecting rhymns and other sacred music. The psalms were sung in course, and standing, regardless of the length. In the most pious families two psalms were sung week days and eight on the Sabbath.

The first book printed in the Colonies was in 1640, The Bay Psalm Book. It had this heading, "The Psalms in Metre, Faithfully Translated for the Use, Edification and Comfort of the Saints in publick and private, especially in New England." It passed through seventy editions. The tunes at first were only five in number, Old Hundred and York being two of them; Hackney, sometimes called St. Mary's, Martyrs and Windsor, which is on our program, were probably the other three. These were gradually increased to some fifty melodies to which the psalms were sung in unison.

Later hymns were sung and the custom of "lining out" or "deaconing" had its foundation in the scarcity of books in the early days of the colonies. It was a most inartistic custom as well as occasionally resulting in contradictory statements, as only one line of the hymn was given. For example, "The Lord will come and He will not keep silence, but speak out". Lined out it becomes these two statements, The Lord will come and He will not,
Keep silence but speak out.

Precentors had their troubles in those days for Judge Sewall records in his diary thiswise: "Lord's Day, Feb. 23, 1718. Mr. Foxcroft preaches. I set York tune and the Congregation went out of it into St. Davids in the very 2nd going over. They did the same 3 weeks before. This seems to me an intimation to resign the Precentor's place to a better voice. I have through the divine Favor done it for 24 yrs., and now God by his Providence seems to call me off, my voice being enfeebled".

Strange as it seems to us there were grave differences of belief as to *who* should sing. Should all the people, or only Christians, or should Christians only praise God in their hearts, while one person sang, and the assembly join in silence responding Amen? However, the congregations did sing, though many had only a few tunes it could sing passably well. Little attention was paid to time and not everyone kept the same tune.

These directions were printed for the singers' guidance in setting or pitching the tune. "Observe how many notes compass the tune is, next the place of your first note, and how many notes above and below that; so that you may begin the tune of your first note as the rest may be sung in the compass of your and the people's voices, without squeaking above or grumbling below". This foresight was wise as in the earlier days pitch pipes and tuning forks did not exist. The book from which our Precentor lines out was the first tune book used in this church and bought by Esther Cowls, grandmother of the present elder generation, in 1826. Old Windham and its companion, China, (Why do we mourn departing friends), acted as pall bearers for many years.

There never was an innovation made in the Puritan or Pilgrim church but a vehement storm of opposition arose in some quarter. This was partly an outcome of the fundamental principle of the

Pilgrims that the elders were the church, quoting from First Timothy, "Let the elders that rule, etc.", which caused some deacons and elders to assert their individual views. Possibly, the price they had paid for freedom of thought and their stern severe living conditions contributed to their distrust and fear of new ways.

If there had been a quarrel when the Bay Psalm book came into use, there was an absolute tempest when singing by note came to replace singing by ear. Singing from printed music was called "the new way", by note or ear, "the old way," and these ten objections were made to the new system.

1. It is a new way, an unknown tongue.
2. It is not so melodious as the old way.
3. There are so many tunes nobody can ever learn them.
4. The new way makes disturbance in the church, grieves good men, exasperates them, and causes them to behave disorderly.
5. It is popish.
6. It will introduce instruments.
7. The names of the notes are blasphemous.
8. It is needless, the old way is good enough.
9. It requires too much time to learn it.
10. It maketh the young disorderly.

A writer in the New England Cronicle of 1723 aired his views in thiswise, "Truly I have a great jealousy that if we once begin to sing by rule, the next thing will be to pray by and preach by rule, and then comes popery".

At the same time we in America were squabbling over the blasphemy of notation and instruments, Bach and Handle in Europe were producing their compositions. It was a sterile soil in which the Pilgrim and Puritan planted their psalm singing, yet it became the cradle bed of today's music.

The desire for better music was fostered by some divines and in 1717 a singing society was begun in Boston "to practice singing by note". Many other schools followed and communities thus were presently not on the same level of musical ability. Those who were skilled in music naturally gathered together for the singing schools and from these choirs developed. Here are some early edicts regarding choirs, one of 1785, "The Parish desire the singers both male and female to sit in the gallery and will allow them to sing once upon each Lord's Day, *without reading by the deacon*". (History of Rowley)

In Worcester in 1779 on the first Sunday the choir displayed its abilities, this combat between the old and new way took place. "After the hymn had been read by the minister the aged and venerable Deacon Chamberlin, unwilling to desert the custom of his fathers, rose and read the first line according to the usual practice. The singers prepared to carry the alteration into effect, proceeded without pausing at the conclusion. The white haired officer of the church with the full power of his voice read on, until the louder notes of the collected body overpowered the attempt to resist the progress of improvement, and the deacon, deeply mortified at the triumph of musical reformation, seized his hat, and retired from the meeting-house in tears". (History of Worcester)

Because of the increasing number of singing schools and choirs, books of music began to be published in great profusion. Northampton, Greenfield in 1823, Deerfield in 1814, and Springfield were nearby towns contributing to the array of books which was almost entirely sacred. A Colonel Warriner of Springfield led the large choir of the First church there for more than forty years, was head of the musical life of Springfield and the great authority on musical matters in western Massachusetts. He included in his collection, The Musica Sacra, the canon or sacred round, "O Absalom, My Son", often used in Old Folks Concerts. Warriner and Andrew Law insisted that the air should be sung by women and adopted the present arrangement of parts which was a very important improvement and one of the most valuable that could be advocated at that time. It had been customary for the tenor to carry the air. We go to Father Kemp for our old songs but that book follows the modern arrangement, (fortunately) rather than the original.

With all this musical activity going on there came to be some agitation regarding musical instruments. William Billings born in Boston in 1746 by trade a tanner, chalking out his first composition on soles of leather was the first American to make his living by music, that is, teaching singing schools. He is said to have introduced the pitch pipe into the choir, and to have been the first to have used the violoncello in church. He was an eccentric man, self taught, earnest, enthusiastic, with a powerful voice, drowning out those in his vicinity and considered an excellent singer for the taste of his day. He was the first native composer of part music. He taught a singing school in Stoughton in 1774 which is the oldest living musical organization in the country. It is five years older than the oldest amateur singing society in Europe which was founded at the court of Frederick the Great in Berlin. The Handel and Haydn society, started from the Boston Park Street Church choir, is some forty years younger. None of Billing's music is found in this church's hymnal, but Coronation written by Holden, a contemporary of Billings, has lived. Amateur choir singing is no where older than in the United States. This came naturally as there were few professional musicians and choirs were made up of the more gifted singing school attendants.

In the Jones Library is a quaintly written constitution of this church choir in 1841 when Rev. Cook was minister. It is a lengthy document but with only 10 months of recorded meetings. The following are extracts from the Constitution adopted: Constitution adopted in Feb. 1841 "to promote our own improvement in sacred music and the most effective support of this part of public worship." Besides the usual officers, censors were chosen to "pass upon the qualifications of proposed members and who may or may not at any time criticise the musical performance of the choir".

Article I of the By-Laws

Each meeting of this society shall be closed with prayer when deemed practicable by the presiding officers. Article II It shall be the special duty of the Prudential Committee to preserve good order within and about the place of meeting. Article III During the exercises of the society, no member shall absent his seat withour receiving permission from the presiding officer and each violation of this rule shall be considered a breach of decorum. These officers were chosen, Harvey Russel, Pres., Chas. Bangs and J. W. Smith, Vice-Pres., Reuben Roberts, Johnathan Perry, Mary I. Messenger, Censors; Lyman Smith, P. C. Alexander, John Wiley, Prudential Committee. Eighty-one names subscribed to this constitution representing the families of the Cowles, Dickinson, Hubbard, Alexander, Kellogg, Smith, White, Spear, Marshal, Crocker,

A Century of Service.

Goodel, Wheelock, Robbin, Perry, Eastman, Cutler, Ingram, Robart, Ball, Cushman, Loomis, Grey, Fish, Hunt, Field, Wiley, Russell, Bangs, Howe, Pierce, Baker, Wilder.

From the early parish records we read as follows: Dec. 8, 1828 Voted to raise $12 for the support of sacred music. Voted to choose a committee of 3 to expend the money for singing. Voted that Ransom Dickinson, Zacheus C. Ingram and Emerson Marsh constitute such a committee. Voted to pay Mr. Johnathan Cowls $19 for a Bass viol. Today's representation of that first choir will now sing two set pieces, "Strike the Cymbal" and "The Dying Christian", both found in Esther Cowles' tune book and accompanied by bass viol. Did the good deacons know that the lively music to "Strike the Cymbal" came from an Italian opera? From other parish records these items are selected: On Oct. 25 1830, voted to raise $75 for the support of singing school and chose Ransom Dickinson, Emerson Marsh and Austin Loomis committee to appropriate the money raised for singing and *superintend the school.*

There appears to be no further appropriation for music until after the settlement of Rev. George Cook when on Dec. 14, 1838 a parish meeting was called for the express purpose of making provision for the benefit of singing. At this meeting it was voted to raise $67 to be appropriated for the support of a singing school for the improvement of sacred music in this parish. Voted that Reuben Roberts, Jr., John Wiley and Ephriam Roberts, Jr., a committee to engage a teacher of music and superintend the school. Voted that the amount this day raised be forthwith assessed upon the polls and the estates of the inhabitants of the parish and the same be collected and paid into the treasury of the parish by the first of January next. Apr. 12, 1841. Voted that the singers have the privilege of occupying the meeting house for singing-school. April 14, 1843. Voted to choose a committee to exchange double bass viols and Charles Bangs, Woodbury Hobart and Ansel Marshal be this committee. Voted that this committee draw from the treasury $25 to carry the object into effect.

In 1846 voted $75 for improvement in singing, Marquis Dickinson being one of the committee. We find this interesting item under date of Aug. 24, 1859 voted that we tender our thanks to Mr. Osmyn N. Houston for the able and efficient manner in which he has sustained the singing and that a committee be appointed to raise by subscription some pecuniary consideration and present to him as a testimony of our gratitude for past services as well as encouragement to him to continue his efforts in behalf of the singing. Voted that J. W. Smith be that committee.

Passing over other parish notes we come to this of March 15, 1871. Voted to leave the matter of the bass viol discretionary with the committee of the Parish.

A melodeon and three successive reed organs followed the bass viol.

The pews used to face the west, the high ornate pulpit being at the west end, opposite from its present position. That arrangement seems to have been abolished during the pastorate of Mr. Cook who writes as follows, "The pulpit was shorn of its pristine glories, given up for fuel or lumber, the audience room wheeled about, a platform with a simple "breast work" erected and the house took the form it retains today. The gallery at east end removed". But the choir still remained at the west. Hence arose the custom of the congregation arising and turning to face the choir during the singing. Will the audience follow the old custom and join the choir in "Coronation".

Dr. Lowell Mason is the chief link between the early American composers and later ones, coming to Boston to take up music as a career the year this church was built (1826). Dr. Mason is called the Father of American Church music. He was a man for the times, plain, hard working, a born teacher who understood the people and could be understood by them. Two of his sons founded the Mason & Hamlin organ manufactory, a third was the famous teacher, William Mason. He developed Teachers' Conventions attended by people from many states who became music missionaries, carrying better music back to their homes. Mason (and Woodbridge) were the first teachers of music in the public schools and music was taught by them in Boston as a regular branch of study in 1838. "Jerusalem My Glorious Home" by Mason was a favorite anthem in this church.

There are two songs not strictly religious, but so interwoven with our better feelings that one hesitates to ignore them as they came out in our middle period. One is one of the best marching songs in existence which started about 1856 as a Methodist camp meeting

A Century of Service.

song in southern colored churches, then became a rather ribald camp song carried into fame by the 12th Mass. Regulars as they marched to it down New York streets, next used by the abolitionists and finally became the Battle Hymn of the Republic. "Mine eyes have seen the glory, etc." Even Kitchiner's men used it in the Soudan. The other song is one of the chief home songs of the world, and belongs entirely to America, unlike Home Sweet Home written by John Howard Payne set to a Sicilian air arranged by an Englishman. We refer to Stephen Foster's masterpiece, The Old Folks at Home or Swanee River. Fosters 100th birthday was this year and he comes nearer giving us national folk music than any other composer, writing in simplicity, but with enduring strength and beauty, a wild brier rose of music difficult to imitate.

The piano group is typical of the middle of the century, the selections being more or less generally used at that time.

Our pipe organ was installed in 1889 and the choir came down from the gallery. The organ is fundamental to our worship in music, and it seems strange that it should have been frowned upon. A Boston church refused to accept the gift of one, the gift accompanied with the proviso that they would "procure a sober person to play skillfully thereon with a loud noise", and the church went on record at this time in this terse sentence. "We do not think it proper to use the same in the public worship of God". Cotton Mather, who believed in congregational singing, burst into fierce diatribe when the organ was inaugurated and denounced the wickedness of Boston. The first Congregational Church to use an organ was in less strict Providence in 1770. The same Boston church which refused the gift of an organ, 75 years later, in 1790, ordered an organ built in London and was probably the second Congregational church to use one in New England. Even then, one of the leading members offered to pay back to the church all its outlay and give a sum of money to the poor of Boston if they would allow him to cause the unhallowed instrument to be thrown into Boston Harbour. It took nearly a century for pipe organs to be customary. An old-time favorite, still occasionally heard is our next number, "One Sweetly Solemn Thought".

A review of the development of church music calls for the mention of Dudley Buck, celebrated as an organist, teacher and composer. In these three lines he has wielded an influence for the betterment of church music at a time when the forward step was most necessary. It may be safe to say that Buck's music is among the best numbers found in choir collections.

Our Centennial would not be complete without mentioning those who have served this church in the worship of music, many of whom have long since joined the choir invisible. One regrets that the list cannot be a complete one, but there is only fallible memory to go by. Instrumentally, Deacon Bangs with his bass viol is followed by the reed organists, Marshall Cushman, Levi Dickinson, Ella Frary, who played for eleven years, Millie Atkins, Annie Phelps Comins and Lila Harrington Taylor. Then in 1890 Fred Graves played the new pipe organ followed by Lucy Bement Sanderson, Harry Wiley, Mrs. Willard, Samuel Parsons, Mrs. Ralph Watts and Charlotte Sheffield Cassidy. One hopes the heavenly home gives a specially fine harp to those who faithfully attended choir rehearsal, year in and year out. These women served the church in that way: Mrs. John Guertin, Etta Cowls Cushman, Hattie Smith, who sang for 20 years or more and is still with us; Mary Graves, Mrs. Sarah Cowls, Ella Angus, Ella Dutton Hall, Mrs. C. O. Howes, Gertie Atkins Day, Cora Guertin Ingram, Martha Wood Ainsworth, Annie Phelps Comins, Della Shumway Wheelock with Ida Puffer, Jennie Billings and Hattie H. Parsons who still live in the community. Among the men were Dea. S. E. Harrington, Seth Smith, Charles H. Kellogg, Edward Atkins, C. R. Dickinson, Charles O. Howes, Edward Cushman, Dr. William Dwight, Lowell & Manning Roberts, Homer Fisher, Frank Frary, O. C. Smith, Francis Cowls, F. W. Harrington, George Taylor, Asa Sanderson, Forester Ainsworth, W. B. Billings and H. A. Parsons.

The giant strides America has made in music in a century or more, from square cut psalm singing and lining out, the proscription of secular music and a primitive orchestra to a land where the best of music is found in its chief cities, is chiefly due to four causes:

1. Advances made in the standard of musical performances.
2. Creation of groups of splendid native composers.
3. Establishment of large and thoroly equipped music schools.
4. The evolution of a good system of public school training in vocal music.

NEIGHBORS OF NORTH AMHERST CHURCH IN AMHERST

John M. Tyler

The first impulse to form a church and erect a Meeting House in North Amherst was probably the fact that the minister of the Church in the center was an obstinate Tory during the Revolution, to whom they would not listen. The foundations of this Church were religion, patriotism and independence.

Anyone passing your cemetery after Decoration Day cannot fail to notice how thickly it is dotted with flags marking the graves of men who served in the Revolution, in the Civil War or in the last great war.

I wish my father were here to give this word of greeting to you from the "Center." (Perhaps he is "listening in.") Passing the house of one of the old families he would say to me "The people in that house were very kind to me when I was a poor student in Amherst College." He preached here often, "supplied" the Church for the larger part of one year; was ordained here; he always maintained that he was Bishop of North Amherst, as well as of some surrounding villages, and was proud of his Bishopric.

While he was supplying here he was suddenly called away one Sunday and had to send a substitute. One of your prominent citizens—call him Mr. A., seeing the preacher ascend the steps to the pulpit, and having an unfavorable opinion of him, "stomped" out of the Meeting House. A day or two later I discovered my father arrayed in the suit which he always wore at funerals and other solemn occasions and said to him "Who are you burying today?" He answered solemnly "Nobody, I am going up to talk with A. about his treating the minister decently." He went forth, stayed nearly the whole afternoon, and returned very weary. I wish I could have heard their conversation, but both kept a discretely total silence concerning it. I know that each of them loved the other better because of or in spite of it. I hope and trust that after the conversation Mr. A was as weary as my father.

I asked him one day why North Amherst always looked prosperous and progressive; it had water power but the soil was none too good. He looked at me sternly and said: "Water power and soil never made North Amherst; it was the men and women."

We, the people of Amherst, are too busy to send many messages to one another. We do not need to do so, we are one town and understand one another, and work together busily building the Amherst which is to be the finest, most beautiful and lovely and healthy and ideal village in the most beautiful valley in the world. If this sounds provincial, make the best of it. We will show others how to build the ideal village and will infect them with its spirit.

Beautiful for situation, the joy of the whole earth is Amherst, on the sides of the north (and the east and the south and in the center) the village of the great King, to whose glory your fathers and mothers founded this Church and builded this Meeting House. "God is in the midst of her; she shall not be moved: God shall help her and that right early." In this great and glorious work, well begun by our sturdy fathers, North Amherst will do her full share as she always has done in the past.

ECONOMIC FACTS OF A CENTURY AGO

F. S. Cooley

Before people can properly support public enterprises, they must secure more than enough means for personal subsistance. It is the purpose of this paper to glance at the circumstances of the residents of North Amherst with a view to learning at how great sacrifice they undertook the building of this church and the maintenance of religious worship here. The faithful zeal with which they have supported the latter uninterruptedly throughout the century is a fitting index to the character of our North Amherst forefathers.

One fact that must be recognized at the outset is that cash transactions were not then the general rule. Barter was the common mode of trade. Pay for labor and commodities was made to a large extent in goods. Actual money came mostly in small sums and with not too great frequency. The harvest hand took for his pay for reaping and threshing a certain portion of the rye or other crop in which he dealt. The miller took tolls on the grain ground. The carder and fuller took a share of the wool brought for his services toward clothing his patrons.

Though the stage of civilization in America where the sacred codfish or tobacco were accepted in lieu of money had passed, people had progressed only a little way towards the commercial basis of society in which we live.

North Amherst homes were, to a large extent, self-contained. The necessities of food, clothing, shelter, and furniture were of home production and manufacture, and were supplemented by exchange with some neighbor. Products of which one had an abundance were swapped for others which were lacking.

The parish was slowly emerging from the home production of all necessities to a stage where cash returns were more considerable, and goods imported or procured from neighbors could be bought with money.

For example, the food of the family, based on rye and "injun" and salt pork or beef, was home grown. Hasty pudding, hulled corn, and corn-bread were staples. Next to corn, rye was the cereal grain produced in greatest abundance. Wheat was not so generally raised and white bread was for company, or, if consumed by the family, it was thought that they were thereby giving themselves airs. Potatoes, beans, and turnips were grown for home use, but not in a commercial way. (Episode of Squire Chester Dickinson, the cats and the beans.)

Likewise, the meat supply was mainly home grown. Two fat cattle a week would supply the Amherst butcher with what he needed for the local trade down to quite a recent date. The family put down its supply of pork in various forms. Beef could be frozen and kept in winter, or corned; and for summer, meats from smaller animal took its place to a degree. A mutton dressing forty pounds was not much of a problem to keep in the size of families then prevailing. Sometimes three or four neighbors took turns in killing a small beef or veal, dividing the meat among them during the summer season.

For clothing, nearly every farmer kept a small flock of sheep. His wool went to a local woolen mill to be carded and spun and woven. Such mills have persisted in the region to well down in the last half of the past century. Flax was grown on most of the farms for the manufacture of linens and towe in the household. Shoes were made by an itinerant cobbler from hides home grown and tanned in a nearby tannery.

Furniture had not then begun to characterize Grand Rapids.

Whence, then, did North Amherst parishioners obtain the money for building the church and to defray the maintenance? For they voted Rev. W. N. Hunt a salary of $450 per year, which did not then include a house to live in. By 1830 the nucleus of a ministerial fund amounting to about $3,000 had been given to the parish for the support of orthodox preaching, and it yielded $185 towards the salary of Rev. Hunt. During the 1830's the parish paid $275 towards the minister's salary and raised $330 for all expenses. By 1838 the fathers wanted to settle one Rev. Corbin Kidder so badly that they rashly offered him $600 annually. When he declined the call, better judgment prevailed, and they secured the services of Rev. Geo. Cook at $500 per year. The amount raised by the parish for all expenses was $400.

This does not seem like a large sum of money now, even to a parish much smaller with a vast increase in non-Protestant families. From Plumtrees and Russellville, and the City, as well as from many homes now occupied by families of foreign extraction, gathered weekly a congregation fully double the present membership. Prior to 1841, one hundred and forty-seven names appear on the rolls of the parish as members. It would require, therefore, only an average of about $3.00 per member to make up the amount of the year's budget. The serious tone of parish fiscal affairs and the efforts of the collector to get the money afford a glimpse of the average tax then which would scarcely pay for filling the gas tank of your auto once today.

North Amherst had a citizenship characterized by industry and thrift. It had also a number of people who were rated wealthy according to the standards of their day; men who by their own genius or through inheritance were well off. I asked the question once how these men became rich. When the answer "selling rum and shaving notes" was given, I did not feel justified for the purposes of this paper in pursuing the inquiry further, even though these men commanded the respect of their day and generation. I was told of one man of wealth, Mr. Draper, who made a practice of putting out pigs to be fed and fattened on half shares. At butchering time he received half the carcass or half its value in money. A Mr. Pratt of Shutesbury took a pig from him on those terms, took it home, and the next day he dressed it and brought back the half belonging to the financier.

Luxuries were not denied to some of our citizens of a century ago, for in my search I found a paper crediting one Joseph Eastman with having paid, in 1802, $6.00 duty on a two-wheel chaise for two years. He also paid $.75 fine for not entering his old carriage for tax. He is charged with having procured fourteen pounds of brown sugar of Porter & Hopkins of Hadley for $2.00 in 1808, and fifteen gallons of whale oil at $.62 per gallon in 1814. His coffin was bought by Chester Marshall May 15, 1816 at $10.00. Coffins seemed to have reduced in price somewhat during the next decade or two, for Deacon Eben Briggs supplied two coffins to members of the Eastman family on the order of Chester Marshall after 1830 for $7.00 each.

The high price of illuminating whale oil is noteworthy, and the low price of coffins; also the fact that even brown sugar at fifteen cents a pound was in the catagory of luxuries. Maple sugar and honey performed the function of sweetening to a large degree.

Having noted Joseph Eastman's affluence, it may be well to mention the fact that others in the community were not lacking in this world's goods. Quite a number of others were characterized by circumstances of substantial citizenry, and the industry and thrift of most of the citizens precluded the appearance of much real poverty.

My grandfather was born in 1790. He was, therefore, in his prime at the founding of the church in 1826. I often have heard it said of him that he intended to have his team earn enough in winter to pay the cash outlay for labor in summer. It will be understood that railways had not become the mode of transportation, and that horse hauling over Shutesbury Mountain to the East, Ware to the South, Hoosac to the West, was the rule. The product that was chiefly hauled may have been rye which was the most important crop of commerce, wheat being little grown, and corn and oats largely for home consumption. It was his practice to sow the lighter portion of the farm, of which there was a considerable acreage, to rye about once in three years. His practice and experience may be cited as typical of the substantial farmers of the time.

As indicating the cash prices received for common farm commodities about 1820 the following is offered: Corn, $1.00 per bushel; oats, 34c; fresh meat, veal, mutton, and beef, 4c to 5c; salt pork, 10c; cheese 7c; butter, 12½c; potatoes, 33⅓; cotton cloth, 25c per yard. J. M. Smith, historian of Sunderland, is authority for the statement that butter was manufactured by the housewife and invariably a prequisite of hers, while cheese was paid for to the farmer himself. Chester Marshall sold his hog in 1830 to Sweetzer & Cutler at 5½c per pound, the carcass weighing 374 pounds, much heavier than we are accustomed to feed such stock at present.

I recall many talks with the late Daniel Crocker* who must have passed his boyhood during the founding of this church. He related one of his boyhood occupations as that of keeping the hens from the pigs while the latter were feeding in order to prevent their stealing the pigs' provender. His father§ raised a family of four-

---
* born in 1814. §Beal Crocker.

teen with a minimum of expense. He used to team his products to Boston in the winter for cash and buying the small amount of things required for home consumption including tea. It is said to have been his custom to shop around the different stores for samples of tea to try out in his room. The samples were sufficient to make his year's supply, so the purchase was unnecessary.

It is related that the second parish bought of Joseph Eastman, April 29, 1820, a fat steer for $45.59½, the hide, tallow, and quarters weighing 829 pounds. Cash was not entirely wanting in those days. It took a horse two trips to town to earn fifty cents, however, and a team of oxen worked half a day for $1.00.

Not until well toward the middle of the last century did the broom industry assume important proportions. It is true that never did it have the importance it attained in some of the surrounding towns. Yet some of our substantial pillars were engaged in broom manufacture and sale. The Howards, Hiram and Mendel, the Ingrams, Lucius, Aaron and Austin, Deacon Lyman Smith, the father* of Henry Ufford, and Alfred Brown are examples of men engaged in the broom industry. Many others produced the brush for this important enterprise.

On the distaff side, a fitting complement to the trying of brooms by some of the men, was the braiding of straw into hats. Quite a number of women of old North Amherst became adepts in the art of braiding leghorn straw hats. My memory does not take me back to the beginning of this industry, but the Crockers and the Balls of Plumtrees, Mrs. Spencer Smith, Mrs. Homer Gallond, of "the Hollow" and others were able to eke out the family income by braiding straw, put out and gathered up periodically under the management of Leonard Hills of Amherst. Thus broom tying and straw hat weaving became important industries of this village and surrounding towns.

In the fall of the year, many farmers and orchardists turned their attention to the manufacture of cider. Cider was a more important product then than now. Pelham, to the East, easily carried off the palm in the number of barrels per capita, but Amherst, including North Amherst, Hadley, Leverett, and Shutesbury, were not lacking in this respect. Commercial orcharding was not then held

---

* Lucian Ufford.

in esteem. Apples were mainly a domestic resource. The number of varieties was larger because individuals sought to prolong the season by the introduction of all the standard varieties and the large addition of favorite sorts grown by their friends. A generous proportion of native stock was produced for cider. The cider mill owned by Abijah Dickinson on the Leverett Road was a community institution. The work of cider making, carried on for years by Abijah Dickinson, was later continued by "Widow Bijah" of Rev. George Cook's time, then by Sam Dickinson, and finally by Lewis Bartlett. The amount of cider consumed in North Amherst was not far from five barrels per family.

While these industries, broom tying, straw hat braiding, and cider making, were carried on generally throughout North Amherst, there was a class of industries dependent mainly upon the water power of Mill River. I have been told by one* who was familiar with Mill River from its source in Lock's Pond to its mouth in North Hadley of twenty-nine power sites scattered along its banks. Of these no less than six were found in North Amherst. They comprised chiefly the industries relating to wood and cereal working, but included paper and fibre as well. One of the earliest was established by Reuben Roberts and Benjamin Cox in 1803. Roberts was a paper maker by trade who was located first at East Hartford, then at Northampton, and finally at North Amherst City. In 1809, Ephraim Roberts bought out Cox and the business was continued under the firm name of Roberts Brothers. They manufactured writing paper by hand machinery. Roberts gathered rags throughout the State to supply their mill and teamed the finished product to Albany. As time went on the four sons of Reuben, Charles, Reuben, Jr., Sylvester, and George assumed the management of the firm. They added another mill farther up stream and began the manufacture of wrapping paper, straw, and leather board, using rye straw to the extent of a ton daily. At one time night and day shifts were run and both men and women were employed. At length it seemed best to shut down the lower mill, leaving the upper one in operation near the railroad bridge. Manning and Lowell Roberts continued the manufacture of paper in this mill until it was destroyed by an incendiary fire on August 3, 1894.

---

* John Willard.

A Century of Service.   25

The row of maples at the City was set out by Reuben Roberts, Senior, pioneer paper maker, in 1826, the year North Amherst Church was founded.

A large paper plant was established at the City by John R. and Ephraim Cushman about 1835. John R. and Ephraim conducted the business for years, which was later acquired by Avery Cushman. In the heydey of their development they employed as many as forty men and women in their plant.

There is a report, also, of a paper mill at Westville in the middle of the century on land occupied later by S. E. Harrington's wood working factory. A grist mill has been in operation for several generations on the Leverett Road north of Mill River.

Following the paper and wood industries, woolen and cotton mills have been operated along Mill River. Thomas Jones and his associates manufactured cotton at the Factory Hollow about 1840 and at Westville a little later. There was also a carding mill and woolen factory at Factory Hollow. The factories at the Hollow were successively destroyed by flood and by fire in the 40's and 50's. There was also a wood working mill known as Eastman's Mill near the residence of Austin Eastman. This was operated by Eastman, Marshall, Cowles, and Hobart, and finally sold to Levi Dickinson. All of these paper, cotton, woolen, wood working, and cereal mills employed at times as many as forty or fifty men and women in manufacture.

About 1855, the New England Protective Union organized a co-operative store on the site now occupied by Frank N. Dickinson & Son. Ansel Marshall was treasurer, Ransom Cowles, Enoch Cowles, Harrison Ingram, and others were on its board of directors. W. H. Smith, an agent for the cotton mill at the Hollow, and later for the mill at Westville, became its manager. Mr. Smith is noted as the purchaser and donor of the gilt clock in the rear of the church building during the ministry of Rev. George Cook about 1845 (it having been purchased in New York City).

Mr. Smith continued as agent for the New England Protective Union, managing its store, until it was sold to Mendel Howard and John Brown in the middle or late 60's. He then became associated with Bradford Field in the store at North Amherst City.

S. E. Harrington, with his brothers, Arad and Milton, and

Arthur Hall bought the wood working shop at Westville of Church, White, and Wiley, about 1860. They planed, matched, and molded lumber for about two generations until 1909, when the mill was burned. At one time they engaged in the manufacture of garden drills.

We see, therefore, that there was a considerable pay roll in addition to the less strictly cash enterprise of farming, and that the income thus produced was adequate to the maintenance of the standard of living and the support of Gospel preaching in North Amherst.

COMPLETE LIST OF MEMBERS.

PAST AND PRESENT.

Original Members,

November 15, 1826

Oliver Dickinson
Hannah (Strickland) Dickinson, (Mrs. Oliver)
Ephraim Cushman
Mary (Eastman) Dickinson, (Mrs. Azariah)
Ransom Dickinson
Betsey (Dickinson) Dickinson, (Mrs. Ransom)
Austin Loomis
Hannah (Dickinson) Loomis, (Mrs. Austin)
Daniel Dickinson
Susannah (Dickinson) Dickinson, (Mrs. Chester)
Orinda (Cowles) Marshall, (Mrs. Chester)
Mary (Stetson) Dickinson, (Mrs. Abijah)
Abigail (Barrows) Dickinson, (Mrs. Ebenezer)
Jonathan Cowls
Esther (Graves) Cowls, (Mrs. Jonathan)
Eleazar Cowls
Sibbel (Montague) Cowls, (Mrs. Eleazar)
Joseph Cowles
Beulah (Walkup) Cowles, (Mrs. Joseph)
Jerusha (Blodgett) Ingram, (Mrs. Samuel)
Philena (Ingram) Hill, (Mrs. Luke)
Henry Weeks
Sally (Starkes) Weeks, (Mrs. Henry)
Mary (Hackett) Cushman, (Mrs. Ephraim)
Sarah (Hastings) Ingram, (Mrs. Z. C.)
Susan C. Ingram
Mary B. Ingram
Susannah (Crocker) Ingram, (Mrs. John)
Martha (Burt) Smith, (Mrs. Elijah)
Jerusha (Cowls) Smith, (Mrs. Noah, Jr.)
John Ingram, Jr.

Noah Smith
Mary (Elmer) Smith, (Mrs. Noah)
Lydia (Dickinson) Dickinson, (Mrs. Walter)
Enoch Cowles
Julia (Brigham) Cowles, (Mrs. Enoch)
Thankful (Montague) Rider, (Mrs. Stephen)
Polly (Hastings) Cutler, (Mrs. Joseph)
Lucy (Cutler) Dunbar, (Mrs. Stephen)
Eliza Cowles
Daniel Russell, Jr.
Sally (Newton) Russell, (Mrs. Daniel, Jr.)
Chester Russell
Anna (Clary) Russell, (Mrs. Chester)
Cordelia (Russell) Mahogany, (Mrs. John)
Ruth (Eastman) Dickinson, (Mrs. Ebenezer)
Eunice (Green) (wid. Josiah Ayres) (Mrs. Chester Hawley)

1827

Louisa (Adams) Dickinson, (Mrs. Daniel)
Augustine Parker
Olive (..............) Parker, (Mrs. Augustine)
Solomon B. Ingram
Josiah Ayres
Lucinda Dickinson
Emerson Marsh
Adah (Austin) Perry, (Mrs. Benjamin)
Martha (Smith) (wid. of Heman Montague) (Mrs. Lyman Gunn)
Rhoda (Griffin) (1. wid. of Silas Ball) (2. wid. of Amasa Graves)
Phebe Caroline (Dutch) Hunt, (Mrs. W. W.)
Ruth (Jurdon) Smith, (Mrs. Jonathan)
Dorothy (Woodward) (wid. of E. Whiting) (Mrs. Oliver Dickinson)

1828

Editha (Hubbard) Crocker, (Mrs. Beal)

William Kellogg
Susannah (Ingram) Kellogg, (Mrs. William)
Walter Field
Asahel Eastman
Sarah (Fuller) Eastman, (Mrs. Asahel)
Charles Russell
Tryphena (Russell) Dickinson, (Mrs. C. D.)
Sophia (Coy) Eastman, (Mrs. Isaiah)

1829
Elizabeth (Wiley) Field, (Mrs. Walter)
Dolly F. Wiley
Julia (Bowman) Delano, (Mrs. A.)
Sally M. Dickinson
Sarah D. (Ayres) Hunt, (Mrs. Z. M.)
Louisa (Cowls) Hadley, (Mrs. J. B.)
Mary (Smith) Roberts, (Mrs. Reuben, Jr.)
Caroline (Ingram) Cook, (Mrs. William)
Maria (Cowls) Dutton, (Mrs. Alonzo)
Harriet Cowls
Cordelia (Dickinson) Gaylord, (Mrs. H. J.)
Eleanor M. (Dickinson) Pratt, (Mrs. S.)

1830
Tammy (Eastman) Dickinson, (Mrs. Daniel)

1831
Chester Cowles
Polly (Cushman) Ingram, (Mrs. Rufus)
Roxa (Dickinson) Hawley, (Mrs. Philip)
Levi Wilbur
Lydia (Paul) Wilbur, (Mrs. Levi)
Lyman Smith
Electa (Dickinson) Smith, (Mrs. Lyman)
Nathaniel Hervey
Sophronia (............) Hervey, (Mrs. N.)
Wilmarth Phillips
Mary Ann (............) Phillips, (Mrs. W.)
Sarah (Thayer) Dewey, (Mrs. Salmon)
Idea (Smith) Ingram, (Mrs. John, Jr.)
Mary A. (Russell) Smith, (Mrs. Moses)

Clarissa (Smith) Goodale, (Mrs. Rufus)
Jerusha (Ingram) Ball, (Mrs. Silas)
Harriet (Cutler) Dickinson, (Mrs. Sylvester)
Charlotte (Weeks) Howard, (Mrs. Henry)
Cordelia (Ingram) (wid. of Wells Roberts) (Mrs. A. D. Gaylord)
John Sexton
Roswell Bolles
Lucius Pierce
Horace Field
Robert Ingram
George W. Hobart
John Wiley
Stephen Dunbar
Ephraim Roberts, Jr.
Mary (Warner) Roberts, (Mrs. E., Jr.)
Catherine (Dunn) Wiley, (Mrs. E.)
Anna (Tucker) Smith, (Mrs. Asher)
Lucretia (Sanderson) Gray, (Mrs. Abel)
Harriet (Brown) Coon, (Mrs. Daniel)
Philena Taft
Francis W. Nourse
Abner Field
J. Woodbury Hobart

1832
Joshua Hobart
Sibbel (Woodbury) Hobart, (Mrs. J.)
Maria (Dickinson) Marsh, (Mrs. Emerson)

1833
Fannie (Stebbins) Field, (Mrs. Walter)
Sarah (............) Smith, (Mrs. Philip)

1834
Alpheus Osborne
Harriet (Paine) Osborne, (Mrs. A.)
Jonathan Smith
Lucius Russell
Reuben Roberts, Jr.
Levi Russell
Rufus Goodale
Nancy (Goodale) Moody, (Mrs. Aaron)

1835
Elijah Billings
Betsey (Smith) Billings, (Mrs. E.)
Annis (Waite) Ingram, (Mrs. Z. C.)

Complete List of Members

Tirzah (Porter) Shattuck, (Mrs. Henry)
Sarah (Smith) Russell, (Mrs. Levi)
Climena (Ball) Crocker, (Mrs. Zacchaeus)
Sarah (Stowell) Roberts, (Mrs. G. R.)
John Kellogg
Martha (Belding) Kellogg, (Mrs. John)
Joseph Kellogg
Joanna (Kellogg) Kellogg, (Mrs. Josiah)
Eleazer Kellogg
Lucius Hyde
Sylvester Roberts
George R. Roberts
Lyman Gunn
Amila (Wildes) Gunn, (Mrs. L.)
Aaron Howard
Creusa (Wildes) Howard, (Mrs. A.)

1836
Maria Ann Drury
Ephraim Cushman
Wealthy (Cutter) Cushman, (Mrs. E.)
Rhoda (Crafts) Cushman, (Mrs. J. R.)

1837
Havilla (Ball) Roberts, (Mrs. Emery)
Sarah White
Fanny Smith
Sarah G. (Pierce) Russell, (Mrs. Newton)
Mary Ann Shattuck

1838
Elijah Smith
Rebecca (Brooks) Smith, (Mrs. Elijah)
Fanny (Hobart) Roberts, (Mrs. Sylvester)

1839
Henry Shattuck
Charles P. Osborne
Harriet (Kellogg) Baker, (Mrs. Joel)
Lydia E. Dickinson
Eunice R. Howard
Olive (Smith) Kellogg, (Mrs. William)
Sarah E. (Sanderson) Cowles, (Mrs. C. J.)
Mary (Gay) Cooke, (Mrs. George)

John R. Cushman
Ransom Cowles
John M. Loomis
William S. Smith
Edmund Hobart
Andrew A. Smith
Mary D. Warner
Mary A. Dickinson
Caroline (Baker) Hobart, (Mrs. G. W.)
Caroline Moody
James M. Rose

1840
George W. Hobart
Elizabeth (Alexander) Kellogg, (Mrs. Joel)

1841
Susan (Broad) Kellogg, (Mrs. Henry)
Olive (Newton) Eames, (Mrs. Chas.)
Nancy (Macomber) Hobart, (Mrs. J. W.)
Betsey (Parker) Ingram, (Mrs. William)
Hannah (Goddard) Roberts, (Mrs. Reuben, Jr.)

1842
Amy S. (Dickinson) Hubbard, (Mrs. A. D.)
Ebenezer P. Spear
Esther (Rood) Ingram, (Mrs. Ebenezer)
Esther (Haywood) Matthews, (Mrs. Elijah)
Martin Baker
Mary (Smith) Baker, (Mrs. M.)
Mary (Hall) Newell, (Mrs. Cooke)
Mary I. (Messenger) Ball, (Mrs. A. W.)
Nathan Sears
Baxter Eastman
William Gaylord
Nancy J. (Wheelock) Davis, (Mrs. Sabin)
Sarah H. (Wheelock) Alexander, (Mrs. Elias)
Lydia Ann White
Mary C. (Hunt) Towne, (Mrs. Amasa)
Harriet (Shattuck) Russell, (Mrs. Calvin)
Thankful Dickinson
Louisa (Dickinson) Greene, (Mrs. J. M.)

1843
Tirzah S. (Smith) Ashley, (Mrs. William)
Sarah Clarke
Mary N. (Ingram) Smith, (Mrs. B. E.)
Orilla P. (Ingram) Parker, (Mrs. J. M.)
Lucinda Gaylord
Julia A. (Field) Sears, (Mrs. Nathan)
John W. Smith
Augusta M. (Rathburn) Smith, (Mrs. J. W.)
Naomi (Ingram) Ball, (Mrs. Charles)

1844
Eunice (Cook) Cooley, (Mrs. Roswell)
J. P. W. Wheelock
Sarah F. (Howard) Bangs, (Mrs. C. H.)
Samuel N. White
Harriet (Chamberlain) White, (Mrs. S. N.)
Esther P. (Montague) Hobart, (Mrs. Edmund)
Cylinda (Stowell) Russell, (Mrs. Levi)
Beulah (............) Crittenden, (Mrs. Matthias)
Harrison Graves
Susan (Montague) Graves, (Mrs. H.)
Tirza (............) Simmons, (Mrs. ......)

1845
Mary (Ball) Wiley, (Mrs. John)
Sarah (Gunn) Cowles, (Mrs. Ransom)

1846
Electa S. (Bartlett) Cooley, (Mrs. Charles)
Catharine B. (Messinger) Smith, (Mrs. W. H.)
Franklin C. Willis
Tryphosa M. (Gunn) Willis, (Mrs. F. C.)
Marietta E. (Bentley) Eastman, (Mrs. B.)
Julia A. M. Jacobs
Daniel B. Crocker
Charles H. Bangs
Albert W. Ball
Ansel C. Marshall
Oliver D. Hunt
John R. Baker

Harriet (Cutler) Dickinson, (Mrs. Sylvester)

1847
Mary P. (Stevens) Ainsworth (Mrs. F.)

1848
R. Diana (Hubbard) Ingram, (Mrs. H.)
Forester Ainsworth
Elizabeth (Lamb) Pierce, (Mrs. Jacob)
Jane L. (Mahogany) Cogswell, (Mrs. M. B.)
Sophia (Grout) Cooke, (Mrs. Phineas)
Alonzo Dutton
Persis M. Cooley
Dicea M. (Ainsworth) Clarke, (Mrs. Dwight)

1849
Peter Clarke
Rebecca (Gunn) Clarke, (Mrs. P.)
Mary N. Crittenden
Sarah Ann Hobart
Clarissa C. (Cooley) Williams, (Mrs. B.)

1850
Charles H. Bigelow
Emily (Russell) Bruce, (Mrs. D. B.)
Jerusha I. (Hill) Ball, (Mrs. J. D.)
Lewis McCloud
Minerva T. (Slate) McCloud, (Mrs. L.)
Julia Ann Cowles
Julia (Kellogg) Ball, (Mrs. A. W.)
Sarah M. (Dickinson) Cowles, (Mrs. Jonathan, Jr.)
Walter M. Dickinson
Hiram C. Howard
William E. Dickinson
Abijah Perkins

1852
Sarah (Gleason) Loomis, (Mrs. J. M.)
Thankful W. (Cook) Cushman, (Mrs. S. C.)
Jerusha S. (Roberts) Lawton, (Mrs. Robert)
Sarah T. (Dickinson) Phelps, (Mrs. F. B.)
Fanny Crocker
Stephen Puffer

Complete List of Members

Mary A. (Lyman) Loomis, (Mrs. Austin)
George E. Fisher
Harriet B. (Holt) Fisher, (Mrs. G. E.

1853

Albert Kellogg
Charles Smith
Angeline (Smith) Smith, (Mrs. Charles)
Dwight Clarke
Hannah (Clarke) Holland, (Mrs. H.)
Z. Crocker Ingram
William Ingram
Aaron H. Ingram
Martha (Ward) Ingram, (Mrs. A. H.)
Lucius Ingram
Iydia M. (Brown) Ingram, (Mrs. Lucius)
Sarah (Ingram) Whitney, (Mrs. S. W.)
Phebe (Cook) Weeks, (Mrs. Stephen)
Marcia (Weeks) Adams, (Mrs. C. C.)
Sarah M. (Weeks) Davenport, (Mrs. I., Jr.)
Lucy Weeks
Sarah A. (Draper) Holmes, (Mrs. John)
Clinton J. Cowles
Jonathan H. Haskins
Edwin W. Shattuck
Samuel T. Hill
Mary M. (Sanderson) Hill, (Mrs. S. T.)
Ebenezer Briggs
Sarah A. (Fisk) Briggs, (Mrs. E.)
Edwin P. Billings
Norman Roberts
William L. Roberts
Frederick B. Crocker
Dwight C. Crocker
Austin D. Loomis
Richard B. Loomis
Samantha Cooke
Eliza S. Hubbard
Adaline M. (Ball) Wiley, (Mrs. Ebenezer)
W. Windsor Smith
Harriet L. (Paul) Smith, (Mrs. W. W.)
Maria S. Cooley
Sanford C. Cushman
Susan B. (Cushman) Cutter, (Mrs. W. V.)
Wealthy A. Cushman

Martha C. Wiley
Mary E. Wiley
Adeline E. (Wiley) Phelps, (Mrs. Robert)
Octavia M. (Wheelock) Trumbull, (Mrs. ....)
Mary L. (Wheelock) Holmes, (Mrs. J.)
Mary J. (Smith) Dickinson, (Mrs. L. E.)
Maria F. (Smith) Phelps, (Mrs. Chauncey)
Ellen E. Smith
Fanny (Baker) Field, (Mrs. Orlando)
Mary D. Field
Phebe (Gilmer) Field, (Mrs. E. S.)
Ellen (Hobart) Dickinson, (Mrs. Daniel)
Julia B. (Roberts) (wid. of Ephraim Whitman) (Mrs. G. H. Olds)
Harriet H. Roberts
Emeline J. (Ingram) Roberts, (Mrs. Norman)
Stillman Hobart
Edwin A. Cooley
Jonathan Cowls, Jr.
Luthera A. (Winter) Nutting, (Mrs. Levi)
Augustine G. Hibbard
William F. Gunn
Almira (Green) Gunn, (Mrs. W. F.)
Ferdinand Robinson
Emeline (Kellogg) Robinson, (Mrs. F.)
William H. Robinson
Lyman Kellogg
Mary A. (Porter) Kellogg, (Mrs. L.)
Henry P. Kellogg
Ellen E. (Kellogg) Fisher, (Mrs. G. E.)
Sanford W. Kellogg
Emily L. (Spear) Kellogg, (Mrs. S. W.)
Leander M. Dickinson
Laura (Adams) Dickinson, (Mrs. L. M.)
Douglas Haynes
Israel L. Wildes
Charles R. Dickinson
Edward B. Dickinson
Lowell S. Russell
Brooks U. McCloud
Susan M. (Stowell) Crocker, (Mrs. D. B.)
Rosanna A. (Crocker) Cox, (Mrs. Henry)

Nancy E. (Hubbard) Harrington, (Mrs. Arad)
Rhoda G. Ball
Sarah E. (Roberts) Soper, (Mrs. H. E.)
Nancy M. Robinson
Erastus S. Field
Lucinda (Elwell) Haynes, (Mrs. Douglas)
Mendall W. Howard
H. Jane (Brown) Howard, (Mrs. M. W.)
Susan (Robinson) Peck, (Mrs. J. O.)

1854

Eliza H. (Hobart) Dickinson, (Mrs. W. E.)
Isabella E. (Hobart) Doucet, (Mrs. H. J.)
Sarah E. (Olney) Piper, (Mrs. H. C.)
Harriet A. N. (Adams) Hobart, (Mrs. Edmund)
Sophia R. (Bartlett) Hobart, (Mrs. Stillman)
Louisa (Graves) Haskins, (Mrs. J. H.)
Lyman Smith
Electa (Dickinson) Smith, (Mrs. L.)
Andrew A. Smith
Juliette (Smith) Roberts, (Mrs. W. L.)
Eunice (Fairbanks) Nichols, (Mrs. Lemuel)
Henry Clark
Louisa H. (Kimball) Clark, (Mrs. Henry)
Amory Thompson
Louisa (Bacon) Thompson, (Mrs. A.)
Eunice C. (Clapp) Bogue, (Mrs. Elisha)
Martha (Newell) Loomis, (Mrs. A. D.)
Lydia D. (Endicott) Roberts, (Mrs. R., Jr.)

1855

Henrietta Field
Elizabeth (Roberts) Preston, (Mrs. Jonathan)
George L. Cooley
Edward Graves
Elizabeth (Wait) Graves, (Mrs. E.)
Parker Hastings
Elisha Bogue
Mary E. Winter
Lucia (Kellogg) Cowles, (Mrs. A. F.)

1856

Abner Field
Wealthy J. (Putney) Field, (Mrs. A.)
Emma L. (Cooley) Clapp, (Mrs. J. B.)

1857

Margaret C. (Casey) Bangs, (Mrs. C. H.)
Nancy J. W. Davis, (Mrs. Sabin)
Caroline (Bingham) Adams, (Mrs. Asa)
M. Elvira (Smith) Roberts, (Mrs. Manning)
Delia A. (Smith) Houston, (Mrs. Lyman)
Lucy E. Graves
Elizabeth N. (Hobart) Houston, (Mrs. Otis)

1858

Sarah A. (Draper) Holmes, (Mrs. John)
Louisa (Childs) Dodge, (Mrs. J. C.)
Ephraim Cushman, Jr.
Elizabeth (Rankin) Cushman, (Mrs. E., Jr.)
James M. King
Susan B. (Cutter) King, (Mrs. J. M.)
Marshall B. Cushman
Josephine (Bassett) Cushman, (Mrs. M. B.)
Caroline (Morton) Barton, (Mrs. George)
Emeline A. (Jones) Wheelock, (Mrs. J. P. W.)
William Eastman
Manning Roberts
Juliana (Winter) Preston, (Mrs. Jonathan)

1859

Charles C. Bolio
Eunice B. (Hall) Bolio, (Mrs. C. C.)
Elizabeth R. (Furgerson) Briggs, (Mrs. E.)

1860

Eliza (Barber) (Dickinson) Hubbard, (Mrs. M. L.)
Jonathan H. Haskins
Louisa (Graves) Haskins, (Mrs. J. H.)
Hannah (Williams) Dickinson, (Mrs. M. F.)

Complete List of Members

Mary S. (Batchelder) Waite, (Mrs. G. A.)
Flora A. (Davis) Bruzee, (Mrs. G. B.)
John W. Underhill
Mary G. (Ward) (Wid. of J. W. Underhill) (Mrs. Charles D. Lothrop)
Lucy (Crocker) Wildes, (Mrs. Israel)

1861
B. Franklin Kellogg
Emily C. Upton
Sarah C. (Smith) Cushman, (Mrs. E. P.)
Sarah J. (Graves) McCloud, (Mrs. B. U.)
Mary E. (Bangs) Roberts, (Mrs. G. H.)
Lucy M. (Ufford) Roberts, (Mrs. J. B.)
Asa Adams
George A. Waite
Harriet L. (Ingram) Guertin, (Mrs. David)
Lizzie E. (Sears) Guertin, (Mrs. J. E.)

1862
Edwin A. Cooley
Ellen (Davis) Cooley, (Mrs. E. A.)
Jane B. (Ingram) Robinson, (Mrs. W. H.)

1863
Spencer Smith
Martha B. (Potwine) Smith, (Mrs. S.)
James Jones
Maria (Kellogg) Jones, (Mrs. James)

1864
Moses M. Hobart
George N. Howard
Lucy R. (Eastman) Green, (Mrs. Linus)
Lora D. Ingram
Lucy C. (Palmer) Marshall, (Mrs. A. C.)

1865
Theron Temple
Susan (Morse) Temple, (Mrs. Theron)
Erastus Field
Henrietta Field
Luther Fisher

Margaret (Moore) Fisher, (Mrs. L.)
Pamelia A. (Mayo) Spear, (Mrs. G. P.)
L. Adelphia (Weeks) Gallond, (Mrs. J. H.)
Harriet (Crossman) Kellogg, (Mrs. B. F.)
Elizabeth T. (Roberts) Smith, (Mrs. F. S.)
Angenette B. (Roberts) Cowee, (Mrs. C. A.).
Julia A. Preston
Chloe (Pierce) Cutler, (Mrs. P.)
George P. Spear
Lucy (Taylor) Houston, (Mrs. J. O.)

1866
John H. Gallond
Ardelia (Harris) Dickinson, (Mrs. C. R.)
Carrie A. (Crocker) Spear, (Mrs. A. A.)
William D. Crocker
L. Jane (Dickinson) Couden, (Mrs. H. N.)
S. Amelia (Dickinson) Pope, (Mrs. F. L.)
James Bowman
Susan (Allen) (wid. of C. H. Bangs) (Mrs. G. E. Lamb)
Nancy (Henderson) Cowles, (Mrs. James)
Tirzah Smith (Wid. of William Ashley) (Mrs. D. B. Durfee)
Harriet E. (Hunt) Rogan, (Mrs. D. H.)

1867
Samuel E. Harrington
S. Emeline (Warner) Harrington, (Mrs. S. E.)
Elizabeth (Field) Crocker, (Mrs. Zaccheus)
Emma (Hinds) Eastman, (Mrs. William)

1868
John W. Field
Julia H. (Warren) Field, (Mrs. J. W.)
Charles E. Wiley
Charles H. Kellogg
Edson C. Cowles
Forester P. Ainsworth
Rhoda M. Smith
Josephine H. (Barton) Herrick, (Mrs. W. D.)

Abbie (Smith) Cooley, (Mrs. G. L.)
Charles L. Hubbard
Ellen J. (Bolio) Hubbard, (Mrs. C. L.)
Henry L. Macomber
Clara W. (Lamb) Macomber, (Mrs. H. L.)
Julia Crittenden
Chauncey Phelps
John Q. A. Wiley
Sarah L. Howard
Robert W. Phelps
Allen E. Pierce
Martha E. Harrington
Frank W. Harrington
Caroline C. Ingram
Francis M. Dickinson
Abbie (Allen) Crocker, (Mrs. W. D.)
Lucius Hyde
Levi E. Dickinson
Caroline (Taylor) Bowman, (Mrs. S.)
Phoebe (Bradstreet) Herrick, (Mrs. Artemas)
William D. Herrick
Linzy Bolio

1869

Ellen M. (Taylor) Ballou
Mary W. (Adams) Kellogg, (Mrs. C. H.)
Lewis G. Cummings
Lorinda (Burr) Cummings, (Mrs. L. G.)
George S. Chapin
James B. Roberts
James D. Wiley
Albert W. Wiley
Frank M. Cushman
Emma A. (Joy) Averill, (Mrs. Philetus)
Jane E. (Southwick) Bowman, (Mrs. James)
Caroline (Brown) Dickinson, (Mrs. E. P.)
Clara A. (Cook) Wiley, (Mrs. C. E.)
Martha A. (Graves) Powers, (Mrs. Wright)
Lydia T. (Dickinson) Wilson, (Mrs. C. E.)
Mary J. Spear
Etta T. (Cowles) Cushman, (Mrs. F M)
Ella H. (Cook) Wiley, (Mrs. A. W.)
Catherine (Sheffield) Smith, (Mrs. E.)
Sophia A. (Perkins) Crocker, (Mrs. A. F.)

Harriet A. (Dickinson) Hyde, (Mrs. C. A.)

1870

Ellen M. (Draper) (Hobart) Howes, (Mrs. C. O.)

1872

Roxie E. (Dickinson) Holbrook, (Mrs. E. A.)
Stoughton D. Crocker
Caroline (Field) Crocker, (Mrs. S. D.)
Elizabeth (Newton) Hubbard, (Mrs. P. D.)
Priscilla Cooley
John W. Smith, Jr.
Emily J. (Graves) Smith, (Mrs. J. W. Jr.)
Esther A. (Wyatt) Eastman, (Mrs. E. B.)
Mary E. Ball
Daniel G. Smith
Laura B. (Clark) Smith, (Mrs. D. G.)
Mary L. (Crocker) Cox, (Mrs. H. J.)
Alfred Russell
Sarah D. (Marshall) Russell, (Mrs. A.)
Ella F. (Harrington) Frary, (Mrs. C. F.)
Jennie E. (Holmes) Billings, (Mrs. W. B.)
James E. Haskins
Lida (Ingram) Haskins, (Mrs. J. E.)
Mary E. (Roberts) Clark, (Mrs. J. W.)
Kate I. (Roberts) Williams, (Mrs. W. H.)
John B. Brown
M. Henrietta (Vinton) Brown, (Mrs. J. B.)
Alpheus F. Crocker
James Cowles
Anna J. (Crocker) Treadwell
Joshua P. Hobart
Julia (More) Hobart, (Mrs. J. P.)
George H. Roberts
Charles S. Davis
Lucrieta P. Marsh
David Cucrtin
John E. Guertin
Wright Powers
Monroe P. Marsh
Hattie S. Hobart
Ella F. (Smith) Pierce, (Mrs. A. E.)

Complete List of Members 35

Nancy (Cowles) Hubbard, (Mrs. Eli) Willis Church
A. Anna (Heeley) Church, (Mrs. W.)
Henry Henderson
Henry W. Haskins
Harriet C. (Newell) Haskins, (Mrs. H. W.)
Ida E. (Cushman) Puffer, (Mrs. E. O.)
Fanny S. Williams
Mary L. (Wood) Wiley, (Mrs. J. D.)
Milton L. McCloud
Mary J. (Smith) McCloud, (Mrs. M. L.)
Etta V. Smith
Homer L. Fisher
Martha A. (Joy) Fisher, (Mrs. H. L.)
Stephen Matthews
Martha M. (Wood) Ainsworth, (Mrs. F. P.)
Henry W. Howard

1873

Ellen S. (Ball) Howard, (Mrs. W. M.)
DeEstaing S. Field
Editha (Crocker) Field, (Mrs. D. S.)
Carrie Field
Catherine (Embury) Jones, (Mrs. James)
William Gaylord
Cynthia (Childs) Gaylord, (Mrs. Wm.)
Mary P. (Gaylord) Hawkes, (Mrs. E. C.)
Mary (Pomeroy) Montague, (Mrs. Moses)
O. Jennie Rice
Ann Smith
Charles E. Wilson

1874

Adaline (Hemingway) Cushman, (Mrs. E.)

1875

Samuel W. Steadman
Sophia M. (Brown) Steadman, (Mrs. S. W.)
Harriet M. Steadman
George E. Lamb

1876

Sarah P. (Clark) Wiley, (Mrs. J. Q. A.)
Henry Stearns

Janet (Edgarton) Stearns, (Mrs. H.)
Mary (Stearns) Ingram, (Mrs. E. H.)
Mary A. (Hartwell) Edgerton, (Mrs. Benj.)
Helen M. (Clark) Dwight, (Mrs. Wm.)
Rev. Dwight W. Marsh
Elizabeth (Clark) Marsh, (Mrs. D. W.)
Sarah (Whitney) Marsh, (Mrs. Henry)
Sarah (Lawrence) Newcomb, (Mrs. Zebina)

1877

Arthur F. Cowles
Cynthia H. (Whitaker) Tufts
Hattie M. (Harrington) Parsons, (Mrs. H. A.)
Lulu L. Lawton
Mary C. Crocker
Annie O. (Roberts) Hobart, (Mrs. F. A.)
Ella L. (Roberts) Stone, (Mrs. G. H.)
Ernest M. Roberts
Alice M. (Roberts) Tapley, (Mrs. I. W.)
Francis E. Loomis
Nellie F. Loomis
William B. Loomis
Cephas F. Frary
Fanny S. (Roberts) Wilson, (Mrs. E. T.)
Louisa (Hobart) Frary, (Mrs. Francis)
Francis L. Frary
Lilian V. (Ober) Vanstone, (Mrs. John)
H. Frances (Dickinson) Lindsey, (Mrs. J. B.)
Mary E. (Kellogg) Graves, (Mrs. Dwight)
George N. Beals
Eliza A. (Marcy) Beals, (Mrs. G. N.)
Clarissa (Freeman) Marcy, (Mrs. R.)

1879

Julia E. (Hubbard) Bangs, (Mrs. O. C.)
Louisa H. (Thayer) Graves, (Mrs. W. O.)
George M. Loomis
Gertrude E. (Field) Marsh, (Mrs. M. P.)
Abbie A. (Waite) Howe, (Mrs. C. S.)
Kate I. Dickinson

Carrie B. (Adams) Nutting, (Mrs. W. M.)
Addie V. Pierce
Allen E. Pierce
Ella F. (Smith) Pierce, (Mrs. A. E.)
H. Caroline (Newton) Roberts, (Mrs. M.)
Rev. George H. Johnson
Clara M. (Crocker) Johnson, (Mrs. G. H.)
Sarah S. (Williams) Howard, (Mrs. H. W.) Hamilton, (Mrs. D. W.)
Lucy M. (Lamb) Pierce, (Mrs. Z.) Ingram, (Mrs. R.)
Emma Phipps
Charles S. Howe
John C. Parsons
S. Jeannette (Cowls) Frary, (Mrs. F. L.)
Julia C. (Dickinson) Nickerson, (Mrs. C. S.)
Delia A. (Smith) Houston, (Mrs. L.)

1880

Howard A. Parsons
Charles A. Waite
Julia (Hamblen) Waite, (Mrs. C. A.)
Sarah E. (Clark) Smith, (Mrs. D. G.)

1881

Mary L. (Lawton) Taylor, (Mrs. H. H.)
Lucy C. (Harris) Browning, (Mrs. W. H.)
Edwin H. Dickinson
Louise Dickinson
Laura Austin Dickinson
Nellie D. (Cooley) Gilkerson, (Mrs. R. C.)
Anne Pratt
George B. Taylor
Sarah F. (Williams) Taylor, (Mrs. G. B.)
Ellsworth P. Taylor

1882

Newton A. Smith
Lorana J. (Nye) (Clarke) Morrell (Mrs. Chas.)
Minnie G. (Sears) Holton, (Mrs. E. P.)
Mary L. (Ingram) Holland, (Mrs. H. D.)
Annie R. (Phelps) Comins, (Mrs. C. L.)
Cora O. Taylor

Jennie A. (White) West, (Mrs. N. S.)
Clara A. Comings
Ida H. (Ellsbury) Brown, (Mrs. A. H.)

1883

Sophia (Edgarton) Hubbard, (Mrs. E. C.)
Hattie N. (Loomis) Herrick, (Mrs. H. S.)
George A. Humphrey

1884

Olive M. (Estey) Sears, (Mrs. H.)
Mary R. (Keet) Adams, (Mrs. H. M.)
Harvey J. Shumway

1885

Nellie S. (Johnson) Harrington, (Mrs. F. W.)
Fred S. Cooley
Mary E. Cooley
Charles S. Crocker
May L. Crocker
Frederic A. Crocker
Herbert R. Loomis
Kathleen I. (Roberts) Williams, (Mrs. F. O.)
Eliza S. (Harrington) Taylor, (Mrs. G. E.)
Oliver C. Bangs
William B. Billings
David K. Shumway
E. Della (Shumway) Wheelock, (Mrs. L. N.)
Henry Adams
Elizabeth A. (Conway) Adams, (Mrs. H.)
Mary E. (Coates) O'Neill, (Mrs. J.)
Frank N. Dickinson
Louis N. Wheelock
Henry L. Nye
L. Albert Whitney
Flora L. (Whitney) Page, (Mrs. W. F.)
Helen A. (Hubbard) Stowell, (Mrs. Joab)
Bertha B. (Phelps) Ingalls, (Mrs. W. W.)
Sybel I. (Hall) Haskins, (Mrs. C. H.)
Minnie A. (Whitney) Hardaker, (Mrs. James)
Esther L. (Waite) Delano, (Mrs. W. A.)

Complete List of Members

Nellie G. (Cowles) Dickinson, (Mrs. E. H.)

1886
Arad A. Harrington
Elizabeth G. (Kenison) Ingram, (Mrs. Austin)
Emily H. Dutton
Elijah Gibbs
Abbie (Parker) Gibbs, (Mrs. Elijah)
Hattie A. (Gibbs) Smith, (Mrs. N. A.)
Rev. George E. Fisher
Ellen E. (Kellogg) Fisher, (Mrs. G. E.)
Ellen E. (Smith) Allison, (Mrs. R. C.)
Effie L. Allison
Grace Allison
Edward J. Allison

1887
Elizabeth C. (Fay) Gilman, (Mrs. J. C.)
Eunice S. (Fay) Johnson, (Mrs. H. F.)
Etta J. (Younie) Cowls, (Mrs. W. D.)
Charles R. Allison
Harriet N. (Davis) Clark, (Mrs. Franklin)

1888
Annie B. (Loveland) Cloud, (Mrs. F. K.)
Frank K. Cloud
William L. Nutting
Edward A. Parsons
Eliza (Hamilton) Purple, (Mrs. J. N.)

1889
Mary J. (Young) Weeks
Ida M. (Fisk) (Eaton) Orne, (Mrs. L. A.)
Jane (Ellis) (Nye) (Smith) Russell, (Mrs. Samuel)
Elizabeth F. Ingram
Lucy B. (Ingram) Topliff (Mrs. G. R.)

1890
Nancy K. (Hubbard) Howes, (Mrs. N. E.)
Eleanor M. (Dickinson) Angus, (Mrs N. E.)
Carrie J. Hall
Mary B. (Eastman) Whittemore, (Mrs. H. L.)

Edith M. (Cooley) Cooley, (Mrs. R. A.)
Esther R. (Cooley) Cobleigh, (Mrs. W. M.)
Edith C. Crocker
Lida M. Hall
Rev. Eber W. Gaylord
Annie E. (Foulk) Gaylord, (Mrs. E. W.)
May E. (Gaylord) Crocker, (Mrs. C. S.)
Cordelia D. Gaylord
Rev. Edward D. Gaylord
Frank M. Cushman
Etta T. (Cowles) Cushman, (Mrs. F. M.)
Mary A. Bartlett

1891
Lizzie A. (Spear) Bartlett, (Mrs. W. H.)
Mary F. (Hall) Harrington, (Mrs. Cassius)
Elizabeth J. Ball
William H. Bartlett
Mary J. Blake
Franklin Clark
J. Grace Hammer
Mary E. Harrington
Almeda M. (Smith) Rich, (Mrs. F. E.)
Mary S. (Roberts) Root, (Mrs. L. A.)
Frank H. Plumb
Clara B. (Dana) (Hutchings) Adams, (Mrs. Asa)
Wallace M. Howard
Louisa (Adams) Gates, (Mrs. A. N.)
Albert N. Gates
Sarah L. (Gates) Howard, (Mrs. H. W.)

1892
Edward B. Albee
Lizzie (White) Albee, (Mrs. E. B.)
Nellie E. (Albee) Tisdale, (Mrs. C. E.)
Frederick A. Alsterburg
Henry Bartlett
C. Frederick Bartlett
Raymond D. Dickinson
Harry W. Fitts
Robert Fitts
George F. Hobart
Lottie (Fortune) Hobart, (Mrs. G. F.)
Ernest H. Howard
George C. Hubbard

Almena (Clark) Keet, (Mrs. C. O.)
Jessie B. (Loveland) Brown, (Mrs. A. H.)
Mary E. (Marshall) Smith, (Mrs. G. E.)
C. Edward (Matthews) Graves *
Laura E. (Pervier) McIntyre, (Mrs.)
Jemima (Kirkland) Puffer, (Mrs. E. S.)
G. Edward Smith
Henry A. Spear
Harriet E. Spear
Martha (Jones) Ufford, (Mrs. H. L.)
Susan F. Wilson
Inez (Thompson) Wood, (Mrs. C. H.)
Elizabeth (Johnson) Dickinson, (Mrs. F. N.)
Laura M. (Adams) Fitts, (Mrs. R. H.)
Alice L. (Russell) Ray, (Mrs. Daniel)
Hosea B. Smith
U. Josephine (Carr) Smith, (Mrs. H. B.)
Mary H. (Eastman) Bodurtha, (Mrs. J. R.)
Mary A. (Adams) Fitts, (Mrs. O. B.)
Martha M. Fitts
Mary L. (Howard) Haskins, (Mrs. W. P.)
William A. Kellogg
Luthera M. (Shaw) Roberts, (Mrs. Manning)

1893

Mary C. (Russell) Cloud
Frederick C. Kidder
Fred H. Graves
Mary A. (Warner) Graves, (Mrs. F. H.)
Nellie A. (Howes) Harris, (Mrs. A. B.)
Mary A. (Shepard) Loveland, (Mrs. Milo)
Edith M. Phelps
Abbie (Wright) Cooley, (Mrs. G. L.)
William H. Ranney

1894

Grace C. (Smith) Cooley, (Mrs. F. S.)
Roswell F. Phelps
Emma R. (Crocker) Woodbury, (Mrs. H. H.)
Nellie C. (Gaylord) Beals (Mrs. E. H.)

Emily A. Fitts
Charles G. Fitts
Fanny M. Eastman
Clarissa R. (Ingram) Kellogg, (Mrs. Chas.)
Mary A. Kellogg
Hezekiah Dickinson
Maria (Bingham) Hodgman
David Somerville
Julia (Moulton) Loomis, (Mrs. F. E.)
Fred H. Gunn
May L. (Pettibone) Gunn, (Mrs. F. H.)
John W. Field
Julia W. Field

1895

Enoch Bown
Mary (Newell) Bown
Roena Bown
Allen March
Albert Parsons

1897

May (Saxton) Bangs, (Mrs. Winnfred)
Lilian C. (Beals) Graves, (Mrs. F. H.)
Harry H. Billings
Susan B. (Billings) Ranney, (Mrs. W. H.)
Mary E. (Kentfield) Fitts, (Mrs. Robert)
Clara V. (Phelps) LaPlante, (Mrs. G. L.)
Mabel G. Spear
Emma H. Parsons
Thomas M. Nye
Olive (Elliott) Nye, (Mrs. T. M.)

1898

Lillian C. (Read) Stetson, (Mrs. Ezra)

1899

William A. Delano
Ellen E. (Tillson) Belchor, (Mrs. Nathaniel)

1900

Caroline M. (Wilson) McCurdy, (Mrs. S. M.)
Minnie A. (Wilson) Shurtleff, (Mrs. H. A.)
Eber William Gaylord, Jr.
Mary W. (Marsh) Robinson, (Mrs. A. L.)

Complete List of Members

Julia S. (Nash) Bouck, (Mrs. C. W.)
Ellen S. (Richards) Kellogg, (Mrs. C. H.)
Gertrude (Fitts) Baker, (Mrs. O. D.)

1901

Helen (Peck) Harrington, (Mrs. F. W.)
Martha (Johnson) Smith
Jessie V. (Crocker) Paynter, (Mrs. H. C.)
Mary (Soff) Peters
Louisa (Roberts) Evans, (Mrs. John)
Helen L. (Evans) Puffer, (Mrs. C. S.)
Margaret S. Evans
Samuel R. Parsons

1902

George A. Billings
Minerva (Ferrabee) Billings, (Mrs. G. A.)
Orson D. Goodale
Bertha M. (Nutting) Lenham, (Mrs. L. G.)
Rena L. (Nutting) Billings, (Mrs. O. J.)
Percy C. Smith
Rev. John P. Manwell
Stella F. (Dickinson) Manwell, (Mrs. J. P.)
Flora (Parker) Manwell, (Wid.)

1903

Emma L. (Bragg) Hardendorff, (Mrs. Horatio)
Carrie L. Gates
Carrie E. Puffer
Ruth G. (Smith) Ruder, (Mrs. F. G.)
Robert W. Harrington
Elsie C. (Ufford) Wood, (Mrs. H. A.)
Elizabeth F. (Harrington) Maynard, (Mrs. I. L.)
Stella C. (Puffer) Arnold, (Mrs. Charles)
Arthur A. Collis
Edith M. (Brown) Spear, (Mrs. H. A.)
Myrtie C. (Fitts) Bartlett, (Mrs. B. E.)
Marion G. (Albee) Faulkner, (Mrs. Chas.)
Mary B. (Mudge) Dickinson, (Mrs. R. D.)

1904

Robert J. Goldberg
Hattie E. Goldberg (Mrs. R. J.)
Lucy K. (Eastman) Crosby, (Mrs. H. P.)
Lena (Albee) Humphrey, (Mrs. F.)
Freda M. (Humphrey) Taylor, (Mrs. A. F.)
Augustus W. Adams
Sarah L. (Thomas) Adams (Mrs. A. W.)

1905

Hattie L. (Goldberg) Waters, (Mrs.)
Caroline L. (Goldberg) Shores, (Mrs. M. M.)
Clara A. Nutting
Frank F. Wood
Henry Tillson
Parna Tillson, (Mrs. Henry)
Grace I. (Powers) Baker, (Mrs. F. H.)
Ina I. (Pierce) Harris, (Mrs. H. H.)
Minnie (Chase) Fitts, (Mrs. H. W.)
Minnie H. (Grover) Holden, (Mrs. H. C.)
Herbert I. Wiley
David Griffiths

1906

H. Marion (Brown) Wood, (Mrs. F. F.)
Ruby I. (Bangs) Wilson, (Mrs. J. E.)
Daisy (Brown) Harrington, (Mrs. R. W.)
Grace A. (Howard) Goodnow, (Mrs. E. T.)

1908

Rev. Byron F. Gustin
Gertrude E. (Holt) Gustin, (Mrs. B. F.)
Samuel W. Russell
Charles L. Russell
Sarah N. Russell, (Mrs. C. L.)
Ella F. (Hall) Pray, (Mrs. F. C.)
Gwendolina C. (Eastman) Hubbard, (Mrs. C. A.)
Bertha A. (Fitts) Kneeland, (Mrs. Karl)
Elizabeth A. Jones
Sarah E. (Olney) Piper, (Mrs. H. C.)
Lillan W. Piper
Myra O. Piper
Carl E. Billings

Edward L. Dickinson
William C. Dickinson
Clarence A. Hobart
Archibald G. Swift
Grace B. (Nutting) Miller, (Mrs. Ernest)

1909

Lucy R. (Eastman) Green, (Mrs. Linus)
Harriet N. (Loomis) Herrick, (Mrs. H. S.)
Florence (Graves) Hubbard, (Mrs. G. C.)
Harriet C. (Haskins) Cushman, (Mrs. W. E.)
Elmer K. Eyerly
Margaret W. Eyerly, (Mrs. E. K.)
Lucy (R.) Fleming
Nellie R. (Haskell) Shaw, (Mrs. O. H.)
Corrie M. (Pierce) Allen, (Mrs. M. N.)
Burt A. Crocker
E. Baxter Eastman
Elsie K. (Howard) Shaw, (Mrs. R. N.)
Clara M. (Smith) Billings, (Mrs. C. E.)
Ralph E. Hobart

1910

Henrietta Field
Luther A. Root
Charles L. Humphrey
Effie B. (Howard) Crank, (Mrs. H. E.)
James R. Alcock
Nathaniel P. Knowles
Edwin P. Cooley
Edward F. Parsons

1911

Edith C. (Hall) Hardendorff, (Mrs. A. L.)
Dorothy (Mudge) Hazen, (Mrs. E. L.)
Emily R. (Parsons) Colton, (Mrs. J. N.)
Irvin L. Maynard
Grace A. (Eddy) Shumway, (Mrs. L. A.)

1912

Emma Pierce
Allen W. Houghton
Agnes F. (Clark) Houghton, (Mrs. A. W.)

Myra L. Hillman

1913

A. Anderson MacKimmie
M. Jean (Ross) MacKimmie, (Mrs. A. A.)
Grace J. (Cooley) Wiley, (Mrs. H. I.)
Walter W. Chenoweth
Lela (Cullar) Chenoweth, (Mrs. W. W.)
Hubert D. Goodale
Lottie A. (Merrill) Goodale, (Mrs. H. D.)
Albert Parsons
Marion (Sawyer) Parsons, (Mrs. Albert)

1914

Ellen M. Hills
Lucy E. (Ashley) Field, (Mrs. A. L.)
Etta M. (Adams) Spear, (Mrs. A. J.)
Ella (Roberts) Stone, (Mrs. G. H.)
George H. Stone
Amelia M. (Peirce) Clark, (Mrs. G. L.)
Elizabeth J. Dickinson
Laura A. (Dickinson) Swift, (Mrs. R. W.)
Jean (Gilkerson) Park, (Mrs. R. L.)
Mary F. Loomis
Marion H. (Stowell) Southwick, (Mrs. N. S.)
Joab Stowell

1915

Harriet F. Billingham
Maude E. Field
Frank W. Harrington
Helen (Peck) Harrington, (Mrs. F. W.)
Francis B. Gustin
Harold A. Haskins
F. Donald Hobart
Homer S. Moody
Charles H. Morse
Rowland Smith
Clara A. (Swift) Dickinson, (Mrs. E. L.)
Lawrence A. Swift
Raymond W. Swift
Direxia Hawkes

1916

Ruth Brown
Harold Nestle
Hazel M. Parker

Complete List of Members

Marion E. (Boynton) Selkregg, (Mrs. Edwin)
Maude (Davis) Brown, (Mrs. J. V.)
Byron N. Buchanan
Sarah E. (Powers) Cook, (Mrs. H. W.)
Grace B. (Nutting) Miller, (Mrs. Ernest)

1917

Evelyn (Kingsley) Rodman
Elizabeth (Adams) White, (Mrs. Sherman)
Lila E. (Adams) Reed, (Mrs. H. P.)
Frank P. Rand
Margarita (Hopkins) Rand, (Mrs. F. P.)
Charles H. Mallory
Evelyn (Gregory) Mallory, (Mrs. C. H.)
Mildred E. Reed
Frances L. Dickinson
Ruth P. Houghton
Roger A. Eastman
Clarence H. Parsons
Allen W. Houghton, Jr.
Charles A. Dickinson

1918

George F. Pushee
Julia E. (Ladoo) Pushee, (Mrs. G. F.)
Mildred E. (Brown) O'Keefe, (Mrs. Gerald)
Florence L. (Loomis) Parsell, (Mrs. W. F.)
Harry B. Swift

1919

Katherine (Burt) Crocker, (Mrs. B. A.)
Hattie May (Rich) Kern, (Mrs. H. C.)
Ella M. (Dutton) Hall, (Mrs. A. W.)
Ruth M. Hardendorff
Emily M. Moody
Almyra C. (Moore) Reed, (Mrs. G. B.)
Arthur J. Spear
Hazel I. Tillson
Mary E. (Norton) Hamlin
Hazen W. Hamlin
Stanley E. VanHorn
Cynthia B. VanHorn, (Mrs. S. E.)

1920

Olive J. (Warner) Hobart, (Mrs. R. E.)

Elsie V. (Meck) Crocker, (Mrs. C. S.)
Ruth I. (Shurtleff) Hobart, (Mrs. C. A.)

1921

Matthew L. Blaisdell
Ida S. (Moore) Gustin, (Mrs. F. B.)
Edith P. (Parker) Eastman, (Mrs. R. A.)
Russell M. Spear
John Gaylord
Lucy A. Gaylord, (Mrs. John)
Lillian W. (Fearon) Sanborn, (Mrs. J. L.)
J. Raymond Sanborn
Alfred O. Tower
Alfred L. Tower
William R. Tower
Laura (Sabin) Tower, (Mrs. A. L.)

1922

Charlotte M. (Sheffield) Cassidy, (Mrs. M. H.)
Max F. Abell
Helen V. (Bennett) Abell, (Mrs. M. F.)
Arthur W. DeNyse
Evelyn (Russell) Hubbard, (Mrs. S. C.)
Rev. Frank C. Seymour
M. Eunice (Jones) Seymour, (Mrs. F. C.)

1923

Carrie B. (Adams) (Nutting) Gaylord, (Mrs. E. W.)
Rev. Eber W. Gaylord
Clark L. Thayer
Gladys (Cooper) Thayer, (Mrs. C. L.)
Donald H. Bates
Clara M. Cook
Cornelia (Ball) Hatch, (Mrs. W. B.)
Jenabelle (Dennett) Howe, (Mrs. W. F.)
William F. Howe
Alexander A. MacKimmie, Jr.
Doris E. Ottinger
Edna G. (Wood) Ackerman (Mrs. R. S.)
Elsie (Clemens) Brown, (Mrs. H. E.)
Herbert E. Brown
M. Glen Stockwell
Oramella (Senter) Stockwell, (Mrs. M. G.)
Cora E. (Blenkhorn) Archibald, (Mrs. J. G.)

John G. Archibald
Archie D. Goldthwaite
Lottie (Roberts) Goldthwaite, (Mrs. A. D.)
Hazel M. Parker

1924
Gertrude D. (Sessler) Eastman, (Mrs. E. B.)
Hazel A. (Reed) Haskins, (Mrs. H. A.)
Ruth E. Holden
Hazel G. (Moore) Hobart, (Mrs. H. K.)
Anna N. (Olson) Ottinger, (Mrs. Daniel)
Daniel Ottinger
Harlan A. Wood
Genevieve M. Burrington

1925
Louisa J. (Tabor) Julian, (Mrs. Richard)
Ida E. (Marvel) Moore, (Mrs. C. C.)
Mildred S. Brown
Lawrence E. Ferris
Verabel Fulton
Beulah P. Harlow
Ethel T. Harlow
A. Belle (Chapin) Howard, (Mrs. J. H.)
Mildred C. Howard
Harry B. Swift
Ida M. (Kibbe) Swift, (Mrs. H. B.)
Henry L. Ufford
Winifred L. Chenoweth
Parker E. Harris

Ida M Rider
Norman S. Southwick
Elizabeth C. Cooley
Fred S. Cooley
Grace C. (Smith) Cooley, (Mrs. F. S.)
Laura G. Cooley

1926
Ada L. (Mellen) Matska, (Mrs. Wallace)
Wallace Matska
Leslie R. Heath
Grace H. (Ranney) Heath, (Mrs. L. R.)
Emma C. (Bishop) Mellen, (Mrs. H. J.)
Mary J. Blake
Austin W. Magoon
Esther N. (Drury) Magoon, (Mrs. A. W.)
G. Ross MacKimmie
Edwin Harris Dickinson, Jr.
Dennett F. Howe
Cornelia B. Church
Marcia G. Church
Jennie A. (White) West, (Mrs. N. S.)
Mildred E. West

1927
Edith E. Benson
William I. Goodwin
Hope (Cushing) Goodwin, (Mrs. W. I.)
William C. Smith
Helen (Shaw) Smith, (Mrs. W. C.)

www.ingramcontent.com/pod-product-compliance
Lightning Source LLC
Chambersburg PA
CBHW061516040426
42450CB00008B/1650